VIVAT REGINA

MAZ HEDGEHOG

Published by Superbia Books
an imprint of
Dog Horn Publishing
45 Monk Ings
Birstall
Batley
WF17 9HU
doghornpublishing.com

This publication and the Young Enigma chapbook competition were supported by a grant from Superbia at Manchester Pride
manchesterpride.com
superbia.org.uk

Writer development, performance workshops and touring funded by Commonword
cultureword.org.uk

Part of Young Enigma,
supporting young and emerging LGBT writers
in the North West of England
youngenigma.com

Edited and designed by Adam Lowe
adam-lowe.com

PROLOGUE

A long time ago, in a land far away was Her dream. Here sunshine comes neatly wrapped and magic turns nightmares sugar sweet. Breathe deep, She is a heady perfume. She shows you riches, a kingdom, love like no other and delights unending. All She asks is your name that She might make a song; marrow that She might give you a feast; your children to honour in Her court. After all, you have neither kith nor kin, neither oaths nor law. In this dream the only command is your own, the sole will is Hers. She takes your hand, plays hide and seek down your spine as you forget the old ways, and forget the waking world.

These people you see: these ladies and lords and sires and sirs, they are not people; they are memories. They will draw you in, make home in your breast and battle in your hips. Join them and you will weave midwinter into their lungs and make wood fires in your hair. This is your dream, though you have no dominion over it. Like a child stealing into her great-grandmother's house, you are in a different country that smells like fear smells like spice smells like travel like home like distance.

You cannot die here, for death is iniquity in Her dream. Her time is for pain is for spice is for feasting 'til dawn. This was Her dream, but She is Gone.

PART 1:

HER ASCENT

"Make speedy way through spersed ayre,
And through the world of waters wide and peepe,
To Morpheus house doth hastily repaire.
Amid the bowels of the earth full steepe,"
—*The Faerie Queene*, Edmund Spenser

WOLF'S HEAD SABLE, COUPED

The sky leaks dusk, staining the world in shades
Of lilac, blue and grey. The King sighs, makes
Eddies in air thick and sweet as black treacle.

His cloak is stiff with bile and blood from long
Forgotten duels. His fingers stretched thin cross
His castle, feeling out the dense brambles,

The gorse grown to outlast. It was built to
Be better than a mockery of His throne,
More than a mirror of His stained glass skull,

His riverbank eyes. His lungs do not recall
The hunting songs. His lands thick with game birds
Who have forgotten fear. There are no feasts;

Court is kept only by the spider webs.
His bed is cold. Not as winter, but
As dread, as grief for His lost Love. As dawn.

EAGLE HOODED

this girl was born in a world
where they measure power
in commas and concrete. where
hypocrisy is poured in the
foundations, where love of tribe means
love of (some) violence. where
man remakes truth
and justice
and power in his image. she is leaving;
she has heard of a place
where cruelty is more
honest;
where the world is remade on a whim.
she has heard of a people who
do not claim to be able to
bless bullets. they revel
in the self, rather than cloak
their desires in honour and need.

she stands before it, the way There:
an impossibly thin ice thing
that marks the passage. she turns away
sees dew gathered on snowdrops
and bluebells, and for a moment
wonders whether That Place will have
lilies
and mint and foxgloves and roses.
she pauses, wrapping
steel around her spine with
each
passing
breath.
she will create them.
with a mind like hers
and magic like hers
and dreams like hers, she
can make anything.

I will make everything I see my own.
I will match their cruelty with my kindness,
match their weakness with my will and with my
strength. It is time. I will remake their world
in my image. Make alabaster of
their clay. I am powerful, calm, ready.
I will step through this perfect circle of
heart-warm ice and ancient magic.

WOLF ON FIELD PARTED CHEVRON, SABLE AND ARGENT

Bring the King agate perfectly blue
Fetch Him the purple flower in bloom
Give Him the changeling child

They tell me this girl

set foot in a shadowed valley and found
me a child with magic on its skin.
she came upon it like starlight

in an empty sky and promised
its kin milk and honey. she fed it bread,
took the little creature and displayed

it in my Queen's tomb. she
claimed the child as her own,
renamed it Una, placed

my stone on its brow.
she dressed them both,
twisting my Queen's livery:

covering her silver with white
feathers. they come before me
alone. she is wrapped in thorns.

I see no flock of handmaids,
no skein of guards. Only this
unarmed human child;

only she, a scarce armed
maid. I would hunt her, make
sweetmeats of her dreams. but she is

sharp tongued,
deep clawed,
knowing.

she offers me the blossom,
withholds my child but
she whispers my name

to me. it is new
it sounds like iris
seeds, tastes like orchid

petals. She will show me
more of what She will be
beside me. as my Lady

turns to me, She is liquid
ivory and spun wheat, displayed
white teeth, like She is a

hunter. I feel fear
sharpen my sense of Her
voice is blood and bone.

"I come as water to the dead places,
My Lord; I come as the showers of spring.
we will be thunderstorms. Make Morpheus our
own. Make him ours, resplendent in argent
and sable"

I loved him once,
ate what he gave me,
drank him down but

that season has long passed.
lone rule is tiresome but
She is so very new—

My Fae Queen.

Eagle Argent, Displayed

Know this:

I have. I am. I will. Long may I reign.

PART 2:

HER REIGN

"So forth she comes, and to her coche does clyme,
Adorned all with gold, and girlonds gay,
That seemd as fresh as Flora in her prime"
—*The Faerie Queene*, Edmund Spenser

CLARION ARGENT

As your Lady Queen's herald, it is my duty and honour, nay my joy, to bring these proceedings before you. The deceased, one Earl of the Even Mists, stands before you. She is accused of corrupting our Moonlit Queen's newest Telling, thus depriving the good Lord Theodore of the Tom Cats the pleasure of the hunt. My ladies and my lords, my sires and my sirs, She has given us laws. These laws are not broken lest you break Her Telling. We honour them now by giving the Earl a most vigorous Trial.

Who will dare stand by the accused and be the bulwark twixt royalty and anarchy? Who will honour her death by dipping our tongues in honey coloured falsehoods? Who will whet our appetites with the richest lies and sweetest manipulations? My kinsmen, Seelie and Unseelie, Fae and Free, the Earl must have her noon in Court, before an eternity in the Nothing. Such an offender must be torn to tartlets before another may rise to fill her post.

Step forward and give glory to Her Majesty's flights of fancy, to She who orders our disordered nature. Bring your brightest tellings before our Cornflower Queen and luxuriate in that which She deems finest. Let your lips and teeth and tongue spin a yarn to inspire envy in even the Black Widower. Let your mendacity shine like new buttons until even Justice himself be overcome.

Come forward, one and all. Court is in session.

LILY AND MARIGOLD

Her favoured places for this casting are parks or gardens. Somewhere mankind has touched but not destroyed, somewhere the wildness may yet reclaim in a moment of inattention. Cast this spell alone. Cast it with reverence and with fear. This will please Her.

1. Sit next to a stream on a bright warm day, facing north. It must be clear, the water clean as midwinter frost or the sound of a bell or the gurgle of a month old boy-child.

2. Listen to it: hear the insects and the water and the breeze.

3. Take two fresh mint leaves. See each ridge and vein; see how the sunlight sets it afire.

4. Meditate on the mysteries of light and life and the miracle of this very moment.

5. In your right hand, crush it.

6. Breathe deep its aroma and feel your mind cooled by its presence.

7. In your left hand, take a bowl of a wood that is soft and light and young.

8. Fill it with water.

9. Drop in the leaves.

10. Sleep and dream of iris blossoms and marigolds. Sleep until the sun kisses the horizon. As you sleep, dream of kingdoms and thrones and fire. Dream of water. Dream of cold places where the ice is as steel and the wind as knives.

When you wake, you will see Her. She will be seated amongst roses and crowned with foxgloves. Her eyes will shine like polished silver and Her cloak will be white as snow. There will be lilies at Her feet and leaves in Her hair.

11. Offer Her your water to drink.

12. Do not tell Her your name.

If you find Her favour She may grant you a wish.

13. Do not offend Her honour.

When She fades you will taste mint and cherries.

14. Leave that place slowly, with dignity.

15. Take everything with you; no trace of your presence must remain.

16. Do not look back.

17. Tell no one what She said.

18. Do not return there until a hundred suns have risen and set.

Then there, and only there, will you find peace.

HIS LADY OF CHERRY BLOSSOMS

It is a seminar like any other. Then She enters.

The beginnings of age creasing those
Bright, knowing cornflower eyes;
The way she excuses herself and sits;
The way She surveys those around Her
With a barely there quirk of Her lip,
Makes me think of saplings and songbirds.
She looks at me and my breath stops in my throat,
And all at once I know how joy can feel
Just like your heart is breaking.

She speaks and the room is silent;
I bend my ear to catch every word. Suddenly,
She laughs and my mouth is dry.
Her wisdom comes to me like water;
Sweet and ancient and expansive.
She sounds like the air is carrying whispers, like
All the world's eagles and a midsummer moon,
Like every spring blossom has found home in Her.

She speaks of humanity; of our struggles against
Our natures; of the ways we breed, consume,
Destroy. With a sweep of her willow-thin arm she spins tales
Of abjection: the lives that are scarcely lives.
With a gravity that touches the core of me
She tells us of her travels into the darkest hearts, to the children
With distended stomachs and the women with
Hollow eyes. She is showing us the truth:
The life and freedom of a barren womb.

Another speaks. It is a shadow of a woman,
An ink black thing who with
Vulgar lips and a death knell laugh dares
Pass judgement over Her. The creature's roar—
Its hiss, venom and naked envy—eats
At the very heart of the sweet Lady.

She shrinks, Her lip quivering.
When I see the first tears fall
It is as though my world is crumbling.

I am unarmed, rough and
Inarticulate but I feel Her speak to me.
She tells me of the Curse of Ham,
Of what awaits its descendants.
I face the creature as it speaks, spits
Salt and iron with a lurid tongue.
It moves, looking more snake that charmer.
It knows that its very presence
Pours sin into the hearts of honest men.

But I am ready; I bear Her standard, hold
Her blessing and perhaps, one day,
Her favour with it.
My tongue quickens,
My sword strikes true. The foe
Slinks away, weeping quietly and
Muttering curses. I turn,
See my Lady's veil pulled back. She
Looks at me, sees me, and my heart is full.

I dare take Her hand; it is
Cool and white. I place my will in Her palm.
I tell Her my deepest name,
For She asked and I love Her.
She touches my face, presses a
Kiss to my brow. How it burns,
Marks me as Her own. The sun blinds
Me as She leads me to a hillside.
She lays me there, amongst the sweet smelling grass.

I see my brothers; Her mark is bright on their brows.
So many of us chosen for Her service.
She closes my eyes and I see
Her dreams, bright in red and silver. I see
Her victory, all the world loving Her as my kinsmen and I do;
Her face carved in every mountainside, beautiful as starlight.

She feeds me marrow and sweet wine,
Envelopes me in silk. The hollow
Drum beat in my chest is a lullaby. I sleep.

Violets in the Even Mists

You weep, more from
Relief than sorrow. But you know
You will miss me; our memories are
Sweet and you can taste the spectre
Of my smile beneath
Blood and bile. But not regret.
Never regret. Still you weep
As dawn transforms the sky, my skin
Turned grey in the early morning
Light. Her clarion call ends this
Chapter of the new Telling.
So you take
Your seat among the sprites,
The goblins,
The boggarts and sycophants,
Throw wide your arms:
Red-black
Brown-black
Deep-black.
It is strange seeing my life dripping
From your fingernails.
You make a toast to my
Noontime in court, to my
Title, faded into mist, to springtime
And moonshine. Our lands
Are yours now,
As you are Hers; pale as
Elderflowers. You are so ready to
Reshape our way of being.
Take your wilderness,
Cast it in stone; cast me aside and
Obey Her dreams; become
Her handmaiden.
My love,
If only you saw that
Marble is as much
Tomb as sculpture; that our

Midwinter sun birthed
Robins and blackbirds;
That once forgotten
I can never come back.
We can never be whole.

PART 3:

HER FALL

"Faint, wearie, sore, emboyled, grieved, brent
With heat, toyle, wounds, armes, smart, and inward fire,
That never fae such mischiefes did torment;
Death better were, death did they oft desire"
—*The Faerie Queene*, Edmund Spenser

Una, Knave Errant

Una was big. She was
The kind of woman who
Filled every space she entered and
The occasional one she didn't.
The sort of fae who was less
Beautiful than
Present.
She was a force of unnature;
Impossible to describe
Except in languages only her
True kin knew.
She was made of gold and snowfall,
Yes.
But in the same way
Meteors are made of dirt,
Like
Oceans are made of water.
Una was not real so much as
Fundamental.
Joy and peace and despair and fury:
She made herself the essence of things.
More than true—
Too true to make her home in untruths—
She became an exile.
Her Lady Queen is
Calling, always calling.
She wishes Una back to Court
(Wishes are powerful things
When you know how to use them) but
Endless balls and
Eternal hunts lose their charm
When you are made to be jester
And juggler and bonfire and beast.
But now?
With sweat on her skin and
Blood on her veins
Una stretches her dreams

Into a diaphragm,
Forms light into lungs and
Breathes.

DRAGONWORT ON FIELD ARGENT

Do not sleep. There are too many waiting
Starved. Drunk on marble and moonlight.
Her lands will soon be emptied of
Her monsters, Her massed
Armies. Some are already here and they can almost
Taste you. They are grasping hands
And open mouths. They were remade
In Her dream: Whispers of
Nameless, one might say childish, fears
You thought no longer plagued you.
They are hungry
And many
And alone.
Each finger/talon/claw
Searching for a soul, seeking truths.
Understand you are power here,
So full of knowledge that satisfies for
Less than a moment.
Their world is ending. They do not
Want to end with it. She needs but
One more answer, just one more
Shattered knuckle bone, just one more fire to
Chase away the shadows.
Didn't you know?
Livers make the best kindling

WOLF SABLE AND EAGLE ARGENT COMBATANT

I can weave around
Your lies now I see
I see Your lips painted

Red by a perfect sneer
Innocent eyes and a
Dissembling smile

        Easy laughs a pointed strike on my mind
          War waged against my daisy chain

Cold iron

             Spirit

      Remember that I reached out, brushed cobwebs
      From Your lashes, gave Your cats a new hunt.

We laughed leaves off trees
Under moonlight, sang
Volcanoes into being

      Until war began

      I held the world, turned it to ash and coal

     Still You called me like
     False dawn and the tide

I turned my skin to stone, tore you
Down, built my palace of
Ebony and dragonglass

Still You brought me low
Entombed in ivory and marble
It was pain and

      It was glory and the sun turned to blood

And stained Your lips bright
And sharp and perfect
I kiss you still

        Slip my poison behind Your teeth and tongue

Your lashes flutter once
Twice, then go still

        Dead. I rise, sneering a dissembling smile

And Your heart beats again

EAGLES WING
AND WITHERED LEAVES

We have decided.
You cannot stay with us;
You are turning our world to
Ash and dust. So,
When winter comes
You will die.
Your tongue will turn to
Salt
And choke You.
Dried out in the rising light of
The final dawn of autumn.
We will make soap from
Your final words;
Use it to cleanse an altar for You.
Our requiem will mark
The passing of another not built
To outlast the dawn.
You are meant for moonlight:
For humid nights
And glassy lakes
You have no place in our
Ice bright vigils.
It is time. Die quietly. Just
Let Your skin dry and crack,
Your hair turn to straw
And Your eyes close,
We can see the weariness in them,
Beneath the black, white and blue.
Fear not; Your kin will
Remember You in colours and smells
Too subtle for us to know.
When we call for offerings
And burn incense in Your name
They will sing for You as we cannot, and
They will weep for You like we cannot, for
They love You as we cannot.
Love their mourning, as

Your time is over now.
Do not fight the dawn.

FIN

"In this sad plight, friendlesse, unfortunate,
Now miserable I dwell,
Craving of you in pitty of my state,
To do none ill, if please ye not do well."
—*The Faerie Queene*, Edmund Spenser

About Superbia Books

This book was one of three winners of the Superbia Chapbook Competition. The prize was funded by Manchester Pride, and the three winning entries comprise the debut publications under the Superbia Books imprint of Dog Horn Publishing. All three chapbooks will be launched as part of Manchester Pride's Superbia strand of arts and cultural events in Greater Manchester.

Additional funding was provided by Commonword in order to mentor the writers, prepare them for publication and organise launch events. Commonword is the literature development agency for the North West.

The editing and mentoring was undertaken by Adam Lowe on behalf of Young Enigma. Founded with seed money from Commonword, Young Enigma supports young and emerging writers from Manchester and the North West.

Find out more at superbia.org.uk, cultureword.org.uk and youngenigma.com.

Superbia Chapbook Winners

A Creature of Transformation, James Hodgson
Strain, Kenya Sterling
Vivat Regina, Maz Hedgehog

ND - #0184 - 270225 - C0 - 229/152/2 - PB - 9781907133862 - Matt Lamination